THE
PROPHECY
OF DANIEL

A BRIEF LOOK AT HOW AN ANCIENT PROPHECY'S FULFILLMENT IS STILL AWAITED TODAY

THOMAS W. PETRISKO

ST. ANDREW'S PRODUCTIONS

CONSECRATION AND DEDICATION

This book is consecrated to Our Eucharistic Lord and dedicated to Pope John Paul II.

St. Andrew's Productions
6091 Steubenville Pike
Unit 1, Bldg. 7
McKees Rocks, PA 15136

Tel   (412) 787-9735
Fax   (412) 787-5204
Web   www.SaintAndrew.com

PRINTED IN THE UNITED STATES OF AMERICA

ACKNOWLEDGEMENTS

I am indebted to the following people for their help or inspiration: Fr. Michael O'Carroll, Fr. Richard Foley, Fr. Robert Herrmann, Fr. John O'Shea, Fr. Albert Roux, Sister Agnes McCormick, Bud McFarlane, Dan Lynch, Dr. Mark Miravalle, Dr. Frank Novasack, Carol McElwain, Joan Smith, Jim Petrilena, Theresa Swango, and the Pittsburgh Center for Peace Prayer Group.

A special thank you to Joe Pisani, who served as editor and who generously gave of himself in order to perfect this book.

Special thanks to my beloved family: Mary Petrisko, my mother, my wife Emily, daughters Maria, Sarah, Natasha, and Dominique, and sons Joshua and Jesse.

ABOUT THE AUTHOR

D r. Thomas W. Petrisko was the President of the *Pittsburgh Center for Peace* from 1990 to 1998 and he served as the editor of the Center's nine special edition *Queen of Peace* newspapers. These papers, primarily featuring the apparitions and revelations of the Virgin Mary, were published in many millions throughout the world.

Dr. Petrisko is the author of seventeen books, including: ***The Fatima Prophecies**, At the Doorstep of the World;* ***The Face of the Father**, An Exclusive interview with Barbara Centilli Concerning Her Revelations and Visions of God the Father;* ***Glory to the Father**, A Look at the Mystical Life of Georgette Faniel;* ***For the Soul of the Family**;* The *Story of the Apparitions of the Virgin Mary to Estela Ruiz,* ***The Sorrow, the Sacrifice and the Triumph**;* The *Visions, Apparitions and Prophecies of Christina Gallagher,* **Call of the Ages, The Prophecy of Daniel, In God's Hands,** The *Miraculous Story of Little Audrey Santo,* **Mother of The Secret, False Prophets of Today, St. Joseph and the Triumph of the Saints, The Last Crusade, The Kingdom of Our Father, The Miracle of the Illumination of All Consciences, Inside Heaven and Hell, Inside Purgatory** *and* **Fatima's Third Secret Explained.**

The decree of the **Congregation for the Propagation of the Faith** (AAS 58, 1186 - approved by Pope Paul VI on 14 October 1966) requires that the *Nihil Obstat* and *Imprimatur* are no longer required for publications that deal with private revelations, apparitions, prophecies, miracles, etc., provided that nothing is said in contradiction of faith and morals.

The author hereby affirms his unconditional submission to whatever final judgment is delivered by the Church regarding some of the events currently under investigation in this book.

CONTENTS

"*One day, you will see in the holy place he who commits the horrible sacrilege, The prophet Daniel spoke of this. Let the reader seek to understand.*" (Mt 24, 15)

Beloved children, in order to understand in what this horrible sacrilege consists, read what has been predicted by the prophet Daniel: "*Go, Daniel, these words are to remain secret and sealed until the end time. Many will be cleansed, made white and upright, but the wicked will persist in doing wrong. Not one of the wicked will understand these things, but the wise will comprehend. Now, from the moment that the daily sacrifice is abolished and the horrible abomination is set up, there shall be one thousand, two hundred and ninety days. Blessed is he who waits with patience and attains one thousand, three hundred and thirty-five days.*" (Dan 12:9-12)

The Holy Mass is the Daily Sacrifice, the pure oblation which is offered to the Lord everywhere, from the rising of the sun to its going down.

The Sacrifice of the Mass renews that which was accomplished by Jesus on Calvary. By accepting the Protestant Doctrine, people will hold that the Mass is not a Sacrifice but only a Sacred meal, that is to say, a remembrance of that which Jesus did at His Last Supper. And thus, the celebration of Holy Mass will be suppressed. In this abolition of the Daily Sacrifice consists the horrible sacrilege accomplished by the Antichrist, which will last about three and a half years, namely, one thousand, two hundred and ninety days.

—Our Lady to Fr. Stefano Gobbi,
December 31, 1992

IMPRIMATUR
Bishop Donald W. Montrose, D.D.
Eminence Bernardino Cardinal Echeverria Ruiz, O.F.M.

FOREWORD

Fr. Michael O'Carroll C.s.s.p.

This is an important book. It comes at a time when there is growing consciousness in the thoughtful Christian world of the unity of the Bible and the Jewishness of Jesus Christ. The unity of the Bible was very explicitly taught by the Jewishness of Jesus Christ. The unity of the Bible was very explicitly taught by the Second Vatican Council: "God the inspirer and author of the books of the both Testaments, in his wisdom has so brought it about that the New should be hidden in the Old and the old should be made manifest in the New." (**Divine Revelation, 16**)

The Jewishness of Jesus Christ, apparently the most obvious thing about him, is quite recently the subject of an expanding literature. It has always been known, but as a vague assumption perhaps, whereas now it is a key to his character, mentality and phenomenological impact on others. God became a Jew.

It is well to bear these truths in mind in reading the enlightened pages of Dr. Thomas Petrisko's book. St. Thomas Aquinas said that the Gospel of Jesus could be summarized in the fifth Beatitude, "Blessed are the pure in heart, they shall see God." The words "pure in heart" are Old Testament spiritual idiom, recurring in the Psalms. Does the borrowing show lack of originality in Christ? It shows his profound identity with the sacred books of his people; through his Holy Spirit he had inspired them.

In like manner the Saviour unfolding his revelation on the future and the end times, quoted, as the supreme Jew, the Son of

David, what he, as God, had taught us in the book of Daniel. In passing I applaud Dr. Petrisko's rejection of the theory that the central figures described in this book are to be taken as part of an elaborate symbolism.. The very realism of the narrative, the dramatic issues, evoked, excluded any such reduction in meaning. This is reality; these are positive helps to guide the faithful in the difficult times ahead, when they will have to live with this reality; they are not merely a stimulus to theoretical speculation.

Dr. Petrisko has shown in his previous splendidly composed and edited works, a comprehensive, detailed knowledge of divine interventions in the contemporary Church.   He has drawn on this treasury to suggest a very fruitful line of thought on what the Lord of history and his Blessed Mother presently communicate to us as related to what we read in Daniel.

The author wisely allows for mystery in his treatment of his subject, especially in discussing questions like a time sequence. If I state my conviction that we shall be shielded against the worst in the immediate future through the Alliance of the two Hearts, I may be asked then why delay on the dangers that threaten. We must see that it is through the power of God mediated by these two Hearts, and only through the power of God that we shall be saved.

One great grace that we may hope for is the defeat of those who, as the author shows, will seek to remove the perpetual sacrifice, that is the Mass. Travelling through different countries, recently, I have seen signs of such an evil campaign, doubt expressed, even by priests, on the Real Presence of Christ in the Eucharist, decline in the priestly ranks - without priests there is no Mass. But I have also seen signs of the revival, the upsurge of priestly vocations in Catholic Africa, the spreading practice of perpetual adoration of the

Blessed Sacrament; some years ago there were 700 such centuries in the Philippines, the Orthodox revival, especially in Russia.

Our Lady of Medjugorje is also at work, a worldwide movement of faith and fervour, fully appreciated by millions, by tens of thousand of priests, by many bishops save those in the country itself—with one honorable exception, the great theologian, Mgr. Frane Franic.

But is the Book of Daniel and Revelation which, as Thomas Petrisko so clearly shows, so closely meets its message, really revelant to the world about us in our time? To have shown this, is one of the many merits of the book I am recommending.

I hope that the author will give us a sequel to the present work dealing with the subjects I have mentioned. He may have to consider another important prophecy, St. Paul's prediction of the future of the Jewish people, "thus all Israel should be saved" (Rom 11:26). When people read and reflect on this chapter they think of the Jews solely. But surely their coming to the Messiah, will be but the starting point of a universal mission befitting the treasured saintly memory and the immeasurable human potential of this people, unique in the world's history.

—Michael O' Carroll, C.s.s.p.
Feast of St. John the Baptist
24 June, 1997

[Note: Fr. Michael O'Carroll is an eminent Irish theologian, who has authored over 30 books.]

INTRODUCTION

Since the 1830 apparitions of the Virgin Mary to St. Catherine Laboure at Rue du Bac in Paris, many of Our Lady's prophetic revelations have been heavenly calls to the world, urging repentance and a return to God's love and mercy — from her stunning announcement at Lourdes, where she proclaimed, "I am the Immaculate Conception," to her apocalyptic disclosures at Medjugorje, where she said, "You cannot imagine what is going to happen or what the Eternal Father will send to earth."

But when we examine the many reported messages of Our Lady since she appeared to St. Catherine Laboure, it is clear her primary purpose is to preserve and strengthen our faith because, as many visionaries say, at the present time there is a general apostasy in the world and the Church. Scholars and visionaries often trace the roots of this apostasy, which Our Lady acknowledged in her apparitions at Fatima in 1917, to the Age of Enlightenment several centuries ago.

Even though the Church has weathered similar periods throughout its history, an increasingly number of theologians and the faithful believe the modern apostasy is not just another cyclical falling away from the faith. Instead, this apostasy is viewed as an insidious, demonically driven movement against God, which will eventually evolve into something unparalleled in history — the "Great Apostasy" that has been foretold in Scripture.

Thus, if these strong suspicions are true, we are living in very critical times, for the central mystery surrounding the "Great Apostasy" has not been whether it will occur, but rather when it will occur.

Closely related to this prophecy is another of considerable importance that can be found in Scripture and Church Tradition: With the Great Apostasy, there will come the rise of the "Antichrist."

Over the centuries, every generation has anticipated the Man of Perdition, and countless evil historic figures, including Nero, Napoleon and Hitler, have been seen as having "Antichrist potential." Nevertheless, all these individuals did not completely possess the defining characteristics of the Antichrist, which were outlined by the Fathers and the Doctors of the Church.

Indeed, since the first century, the Church has accumulated a reservoir of writings dealing with these prophecies. Almost all the early Fathers wrote about the "end times," and many medieval Doctors of the Church upheld and expanded these teachings. There have also been numerous prophecies from saints, mystics and visionaries concerning the Great Apostasy and the Antichrist, so many in fact, that it would be virtually impossible to accumulate a summary of them in one text.

In our times, more opinions have been surfacing about the Great Apostasy and the rise of the Antichrist. The revelations of some modern visionaries even refer to an imminent fulfillment of these traditional prophecies. Several books have focused on the historical and theological basis of these prophecies as outlined by Scripture and Church Tradition, and some have addressed whether prophecies of the last half century corroborate or contradict what are believed to be the prerequisite conditions for the rise of the Antichrist.

Yet, despite what modern visionaries proclaim and many of the faithful suspect, some well-documented books have concluded the Antichrist will "probably not come" in the near future, which is loosely defined as before the year 2000, largely because some important conditions appear to be still unfulfilled. The most notable requirement, based on a preponderance of scholarly opinion over the centuries, is that the prophesied "Era of Peace" must occur before the Antichrist rises to power in the world.

The Era of Peace, of course, has not yet occurred, and it is difficult to imagine how the Antichrist could come in the short period before the arrival of the new millennium.

Nevertheless, it must be noted that some argue that the "seals" on the "end times" mysteries have prevented anyone, including the Fathers and Doctors of the Church, from profoundly understanding how and when these prophecies will unfold. And because these are not doctrinal areas, no one can say with certainty what could possibly happen in the next few years.

The purpose of this little book is not to argue for or against the imminent arrival of the Great Apostasy and the Antichrist, but to review the conditions necessary for these prophecies to be fulfilled and to then examine how they will fulfill the ancient prophecy of the Old Testament figure Daniel.

According to Scripture, the prophet Daniel foretold that with the rise of the Antichrist there will come "the abolishment of the daily Sacrifice" for "twelve hundred and ninety days" — and with the fulfillment of this prophecy, according to Church scholars throughout history, the Holy Catholic Church would greatly suffer. For Daniel's words concerning the "abolishment of the Sacrifice" have always been interpreted to be a reference to the coming, almost universal suppression of the Holy Sacrifice of the Mass!

To this day, our understanding of this prophecy remains the same, according to experts on eschatology. Desmond A. Birch, in his book, *Trial, Tribulation & Triumph*, (Queenship Publishing Company, Santa Barbara, CA., 1996) thoroughly documents the writings of the Church Fathers and Doctors concerning the "end times" and says that Tradition, Scripture and private prophecy tell us the "Antichrist shall abolish the holy Sacrament of the Altar," (the Mass) and that "this is part of the Scriptural abomination of desolation."[1]

Since the 1980s, the Blessed Mother has said in her private revelations that she wants the faithful to become more knowledgeable about the specific meaning of this prophecy, because with the suppression of the Holy Sacrifice of the Mass by the Antichrist, there will come to fulfillment what Christ warned about in Matthew 24: 15, when He said, **"One day, you will see in the holy place he who commits the horrible sacrilege. The prophet Daniel spoke of this: Let the reader seek to understand."**

Even though great theologians such as Cardinal John Henry Newman and St. Alphonsus Liguori upheld the traditional meaning of Daniel's prophetic words, 20th century biblical scholars reduce the prophecies of the Book of Revelation and the Book of Daniel to almost pure symbolism. Moreover, as Our Lady's messages indicate, the present generation knows little about the meaning of this ominous forewarning. Indeed, as one author observed, we are oblivious of a crucial "sign of the times."

With a renewed understanding of this prophecy, I hope and pray the faithful will become ever-vigilant and protective of the Church's sacred mysteries — regardless of when the Antichrist appears on earth. Most of all, I pray that our generation will respond appropriately to God's call to remain strong and secure in our faith, so that Mary's Triumph and the Era of Peace can arrive to rescue our troubled world.

CHAPTER ONE

THE BOOK OF DANIEL

The Book of Daniel, scholars say, takes its name not from the author, but from its hero. Daniel, whose name means the "Judgment of God" or "God is my Judge," was born of the royal blood of the kings of Judah. Early in his life around 606 B.C., Daniel was taken captive and carried off to Babylon, where he is believed to have lived until 538 B.C.

Through his God-given supernatural wisdom and his power to interpret dreams, Daniel rose to a ruling position in the province of Babylon, much as Joseph had done before him in Egypt. Daniel was so renowned for his knowledge that among the Babylonians there was a proverb — "As wise as Daniel" (Ezek 28:3). Moreover, Daniel's holiness was so profound that it was recognized from his childhood, and Scripture says when he was still a young man, Daniel was joined by the "Spirit of God with Noah and Job" as the three persons most renowned for virtue and sanctity. (Ezek 14)

The Book of Daniel is believed to have been composed during the 2nd century B.C. In the narrative, Daniel is credited with numerous achievements in addition to his interpretation of dreams, such as explaining the mysterious handwriting that appeared on the wall during a banquet given by King Belshazzar. (Dan 5)

Most of all, it is Daniel's famous close encounter with death in the lions' den (Dan 6) that gives his name its popular recognition today. Defiant of a royal decree, Daniel is sent to the lions' den, but is saved by divine intervention.

But it is, of course, Daniel's extraordinary interpretations of King Nebuchadnezzar's dreams and his prophetic visions that have ensured his place in both Jewish and Christian literature over the centuries. Even though Daniel lived at courtside in Babylon and achieved a high station in the ancient world, the Hebrews did not commonly number him among the prophets; however, his many predictions indicate he deserves the title. Indeed, Christ himself says as much in Matthew's Gospel.

Originally handed down in Hebrew and Aramaic, the Book of Daniel, is considered a major example of the "apocalyptic litera-ture," which developed after the fall of Babylon and the restoration of the Judeans to their homeland. What distinguishes it from earlier prophetic writings is that it contains interpretive characteristics of the earlier material. We read in Daniel that the "wise were versed in every branch of wisdom," including the "study of the prophets."

This type of writing enjoyed its greatest popularity from 200 B.C. to 100 A.D., which is another reason the early Church Fathers so clearly identified Daniel's writings in their interpretations of Christ's teachings and the eschatological pronouncements of the apostles and disciples.

The Book of Daniel is divided in two parts: Chapters One through Six relate five stories involving Daniel and one with his friends. The second section describes four visions Daniel received.

The early Christian writers believed Daniel's visions had great relevance to Christ's teachings because Daniel's apocalyptic imag-ery contained the best elements of Christ's prophetic teaching: the insistence on proper conduct, divine control over events, and the certainty that the Kingdom of God would eventually triumph.

Indeed, it is the arrival of God's Kingdom that is the central theme of the synoptic Gospels.

Likewise, Daniel's visions were extremely important to the Fathers of the Church, largely because many elements were strikingly consistent with the Gospels and early writings of the disciples, including the prominence of angels, predictions about the future, especially the "end times," and the mention of a final judgment. The parallel language of these writings convinced the Fathers that the life and mission of Jesus Christ, the Messiah, was the fulfillment of Old Testament prophecies, particularly those contained in the Book of Daniel.

The specific language used in Daniel clearly illustrates the relationship between his visions and the prophetic elements of the Gospels and St. John's visions in the Book of Revelation, scholars say. In fact, according to one author, the Book of Daniel appears to be quoted 45 times in the Apocalypse. This gesture of St. John is thought to be deliberate because he believed his revelations complemented Daniel's. For the early Fathers, references to the "Son of Man," "ten horns" and "beasts" affirmed the correlation between the prophetic elements of the Book of Daniel and the Gospels and the Book of Revelation.

For our purposes, it is especially significant that the apostles and the Church Fathers believed Daniel's writings also referred to the coming of the Man of Sin — the Antichrist. For in that conclusion, the Fathers offered, as we shall later review, their own interpretation of Daniel's prediction of "abolishment of the Sacrifice" with what the New Testament later emphasized about the reign of the Antichrist, and especially Christ's specific warning in Matthew 24. (Note: scholars say that Christ is also referring to Daniel in Mark 13 and Luke 21.)

In his book, *The Antichrist,* Fr. Vincent P. Miceli, S.J., a theologian and former professor at the Gregorian and Angelicum Universities in Rome, correlated definitions of the Antichrist from definitions in the New Testament and the Book of Daniel. Writes Fr. Miceli:

> St. John the Evangelist distinguishes the Antichrist from all other adversaries of Christ. Moreover, Sacred Scripture imprints upon the mind, even after allowing for the figurative character of prophetic language, the strong impression that the Antichrist is to be an individual man. Consider this passage:

> "That day shall not come, except there come a falling away first, and that of sin be revealed, the son of perdition, who is the adversary and rival of all that is called God or worshipped; so that he sits as God in the Temple of God, proclaiming himself to be God. ... Then shall that wicked one be revealed, whom the Lord shall consume with the spirit of his mouth, and shall destroy with the brightness of his coming ... whose coming is after the working of Satan, with all powers and lying wonders."

Now consider this passage from Daniel:

> "Another shall rise after them, and he shall be diverse from the first, and he shall subdue three kings. And he shall speak great words against the Most High, and shall wear out the saints of the Most High, and think to change times and laws: and they shall be given into his hand until a time and times and the dividing of time. But the judgment shall sit, and they shall take away his domination, to consume and destroy it unto the end."

And Daniel once more:

"In his estate shall stand up a vile person, to whom they shall give the honor of the kingdom; but he shall come in peaceably and obtain the kingdom of flatteries. ... And such as do wickedly against the covenant shall be corrupt by flatteries; but the people that do know their God shall be strong and do exploits. ... And the king shall do according to his will; and he shall exalt himself and magnify himself above every god, and shall speak marvelous things against the God of gods, and shall prosper until the indignation be accomplished."

And in much the same vein, St. John the Evangelist writes:

"There was given him a mouth speaking great things and blasphemies; and power was given unto him to continue forty-two months. And he opened his mouth in blasphemy against God, to blaspheme His name and His tabernacle and them that dwell in Heaven. And it was given unto him to make war with the saints, and to overcome them; and power was given him over all kindred and tongues and nations. And all that dwell upon the earth shall worship him, whose names are not written in the Book of Life of the Lamb slain from the foundation of the world."

Adds Fr. Miceli:

"Such specific personal titles and characteristics cannot refer to an abstract ethical force for evil, or to a collective body or movements of evil. An individual is specifically pointed out and identified by his supreme capacity and stunningly unique career in the pursuit of evil. He is the ultimate culmination of all wicked precursors in the perpetration of evil against God and Christ. This man of sin will combine in himself all the malice and wicked art found in all previous evil persons. All the Fathers and theologians unanimously concur in this belief that the Antichrist will be an individual person. In fact Bellarmine and Suarez, two famous Jesuit theologians — Bellarmine being also a saint and Doctor of the Church — teach that the personal existence of the Antichrist must be considered an object of divine faith."

Fr. Miceli also writes:

"When one has studied the image of the Antichrist in St. Paul's Second Epistle to the Thessalonians, one easily recognizes the "man of sin" in the "little horn," which the prophet Daniel describes as a great power arising from a "fourth beast, terrible and wonderful and exceedingly strong," which he saw in a vision at night.

"And behold eyes like the eyes of man were in this horn, and a mouth speaking great things. I beheld till thrones were placed and the Ancient of Days sat. ... The judgment sat and the books were opened. I beheld because of the voice of the great words which that horn spoke. ... And that horn was created, then the rest of the horns. I beheld and lo, that horn made war against the saints, and prevailed over them. ... And he shall speak words against the High One, and shall crush the saints of the Most High; and he shall think himself able to change times and laws, and they shall be delivered into his hands until a time, and times and half a time. And the judgment shall sit that his power may be taken away, and be broken into pieces and perished even to the end.

Fr. Miceli concludes:

> "Now, Scriptural exegetes are agreed that the ten horns on the head of the fourth beast seen by the Prophet Daniel represent ten kingdoms, idolatrous successors of Alexander the Great's Empire who persecuted the Chosen People of God. The angel in the Apocalypse explains a similar vision to St. John thus:

> "And the ten horns that you saw are ten kinds who ... will receive authority as kings for one hour with the beast. They will fight against the Lamb."

> But the "little horn" which brings down three of the other kingdoms is commonly understood to be the Antichrist..."

Fr. Miceli's writings are rare in an age when most contemporary scholars have reduced the writings of the Book of Daniel and the Book of Revelation to pure symbolism.

Likewise, contemporary scholars have tried to replace the belief in the Antichrist as an individual with the view that the Antichrist is actually a "spiritual movement" or an array of circumstances involving immoral and un-Christian parties, which throughout history repeatedly oppose the Church's teachings in the world.

However, the Fathers and Doctors of the Church did not adhere to this school of thought, and they consistently defined the Antichrist as a man with a soul, a man who will emerge when the exact conditions are fulfilled. Moreover, this teaching has been upheld in Our Lady's reported revelations to contemporary visionaries.

Entire texts have been written about what Church Fathers and Doctors have propounded regarding the Antichrist and the circumstances that will lead to his coming. We will briefly summarize what the world will be like when the Man of Perdition rises to power.

CHAPTER TWO

THE MAN OF SIN

In our century alone, three popes have commented on the eventual rise of the Antichrist: Pius X, Paul VI and John Paul II. This is not surprising since throughout history there has always been talk of his arrival.

St. Paul's Second Letter to the Thessalonians provides one of the clearest references in Scripture to the coming of the Antichrist. Paul wrote:

> Let no one seduce you, no matter how. Since the mass apostasy has not yet occurred nor the man of lawlessness been revealed — that son of perdition and adversary who exalts himself above every so-called god proposed for worship, he who seats himself in God's temple and even declares himself to be God — do you not remember how I used to tell you about these things when I was still with you? You know what restrains him until he shall be revealed in his own time. The secret force of lawlessness is already at work, mind you, but there is one who holds him back until that restrainer shall be taken from the scene.
>
> Thereupon the lawless one will be revealed, and the Lord Jesus will destroy him with the breath of His mouth and annihilate him by manifesting His own presence. This lawless one will appear as part of the workings of Satan, accompanied by all the power and signs and wonders at the disposal of falsehood — by every seduction the wicked can devise for those destined to ruin because they have

not opened their hearts to the truth in order to be saved. Therefore, God is sending upon them a perverse spirit which leads them to give credence to falsehood, so that all who have not believed the truth but have delighted in evil-doing will be condemned. (2 Th 2: 3-12)

The Gospel according to Saint Matthew also depicts his coming: "One day, you will see in the holy place he who commits the horrible sacrilege. The prophet Daniel spoke of this. Let the reader seek to understand." (Mt 24:15)

Likewise, *The Catechism of the Catholic Church*, published in 1994, states:

"Before Christ's second coming, the Church must pass through a final trial that will shake the faith of many believers. The persecution that accompanies her pilgrimage on earth will unveil the "mystery of iniquity" in the form of a religious deception offering men an apparent solution to their problems at the price of apostasy from the truth. The supreme religious deception is that of the Antichrist, a pseudo-messianism by which man glorifies himself in place of God and of his Messiah come in the flesh.

The Antichrist's deception already begins to take shape in the world every time the claim is made to realize within history that messianic hope which can only be realized beyond history through the eschatological judgment. The Church has rejected even modified forms of this falsification of the kingdom to come under the name of millenarianism, especially the "intrinsically perverse" political form of a secular messianism.

The Church will enter the glory of the kingdom only through this final Passover, when she will follow her Lord in his Death and Resurrection. The kingdom will be fulfilled, then, not by a historic triumph of the Church through a progressive ascendancy, but only by God's victory over the final unleashing of evil, which will cause his Bride to come down from heaven. God's triumph over the revolt of evil will take form of the Last Judgment after the final cosmic upheaval of this passing world."

The word "Antichrist" is composed of two Greek words, "anti," meaning "against," and "xristos," meaning "Christ." In addition to the term, "Antichrist," the Bible also refers to him as the "man of sin," "the son of perdition," "the beast," and "the lawless one." Little seems to be known of him, other than the number obtained from the addition of the Greek letters of his name will be "666."

Author Michael Freze, in his book *Voices, Visions, Apparitions* offers this definition of the Antichrist:

> "The one who is to come during the hour of the Great Tribulation, the embodiment of pure evil. The Antichrist will be a real person who represents the forces of Satan in the cosmic battle between Christ and the demons at the end of time. Although many "Antichrists" have appeared throughout the ages (1 Jn 2:18), the Scriptures remind us that there is indeed a personal, evil being who will one day be possessed by the devil with the intentions of destroying the world: '... the devil has come down to you in great wrath, because he knows that his time is short!'" (Rev 12:12)

Today, as in previous centuries, the primary question surrounding the Antichrist is: "When will this dreadful individual come?" As with the birth of Christ, specific conditions have been established for his appearance, which is only subject to the "signs" of his impending arrival.

Over the years, many writers have attempted to define these signs or circumstances, and have outlined certain conditions that must exist, according to Scripture and Tradition.

In summary, the Antichrist will come when the whole world renounces the teachings of Christ and rejects the authority of His Church, and when men shall say as they said of Jesus, "We will not have this man reign over us" (Lk 19:14), and "We have no king, but Caesar." (Jn 19:15)

As the Catechism states, the Holy Catholic Church will then pass through a great persecution, and many scholars agree that this period will make all previous trials seem insignificant. As far back as the 4th century, St. Augustine wrote that these persecutions will "be violent, like those against the early Christians." Additionally, there will be the deception of false brethren.

The combination of these two persecutions will prove more terrible than either alone, and even though precursors of the lawless one have existed in almost every century, experts say the Antichrist will not appear until there is widespread heresy, apostasy, and schism, along with incredulity and impiousness in which many "will give themselves up to their passions and drink from the pool of iniquity."

Throughout the centuries, theologians have maintained that worldwide political antecedents, along with religious ones, must also occur before the Antichrist can appear. This means that virtually all intellectual and moral reasoning in the world must reach the point at which prevailing thought "contradicts all good."

These circumstances will then create a vacuum — quite simply the world will hunger for a philosophy and an authority, and at that time, a new authority will replace Christianity, but it will consist of a Babel of absurd ideas that will lead to rampant perversion, which will find the world in the grip of ... the Antichrist.

Once he is in power, his reign will be a brief period of horror and suffering unlike any before, especially for Christians. Church Fathers and Doctors have written detailed accounts of what they understand this trial to entail. And their understanding is believed to be directly handed down from the apostles and disciples of Christ.

Most significantly, the reign of the Antichrist will fulfill the words of the prophet Daniel (Dan 12:9-12), who foretold these events and whose prophecies Christ himself reiterated (Mt 24:15) — that a certain individual would arise to power one day to commit "the horrible abomination," a great sacrilege that has always been understood to be related to the Church.

But although Catholic writers have concurred over the centuries on the meaning of Daniel's prophecy and its fulfillment perhaps for the first time we also find visionaries and mystics warning of the prophecy's impending fulfillment.

Therefore, even though much of this prophetic unfolding remains a mystery in our time, it is necessary for us to examine Daniel's words and what previous Catholic writers have understood them to mean. In this way, we will be better able to interpret what visionaries are revealing concerning the fulfillment of this ancient prophecy.

CHAPTER THREE

AN ANCIENT PROPHECY

It has been 2,000 years since Christ warned of the fulfillment of Daniel's prophecies, and during the past half-century, visionaries have increasingly issued warnings, which are believed to be from Jesus and Mary and which suggest the Sacrifice of the Mass and the True Presence of Jesus Christ in the Eucharist are in danger of being suppressed.

These are extraordinary warnings, and we have to wonder what they really mean. What exactly is this "danger"? How could it happen?

Even though it is well-documented that many visionaries are foretelling an attack on the Church's sacred mysteries, particularly the Sacrifice of the Mass, it is important to remember that many of these visionaries also say the Mass will never be totally suppressed and that a great victory by God is at hand. Indeed, this predicted victory will solidify Christ's Eucharistic Presence throughout the world.

Nevertheless, visionaries say that when suppression of the Mass occurs, the effect on the Church and the world will be more tumultuous than any other oppression in history, even the French Revolution during the late 18th century and the Communist tyrannies of the 20th century.

Some writers believe this prophecy is connected to the apostasy foretold by the Blessed Virgin Mary at Fatima and Akita, an apostasy that is still unfolding and is expected to be the climax of the assault on the Church which has been occurring for hundreds of years.

The Rev. Msgr. Richard L. Carroll, V.F. gives us this summary in his 1993 book, *The Remnant Church*. Fr. Carroll writes:

> It must sadden the heart of Our Lord Jesus at the indifference of so many Catholics. Constantly, Our Lady has urged us to make the Mass the central act of our life. I believe one of the trials during the purification will center on the Mass and the Eucharist and of the denial of the Real Presence.

Several years later in 1996, Fr. Carroll issued a similar warning in his book, *The Third Millennium and The Triumph of Our Lady:*

> We know that Our Blessed Mother has warned us as early as Fatima in 1917, and again in Medjugorje, of trials that will beset the Church.
>
> I believe that in the time of trial, the last heresy will be denial of the Real Presence of Jesus in the Eucharist. The great hope of the Church will be the Remnant Communities — those who not only believe in the Real Presence of Jesus in the Eucharist, but who demonstrate the belief by Perpetual Adoration of the Blessed Sacrament.

It would not be possible to quote all the visionaries in this century, or even half-century, who have warned of a suppression of the Mass; however, since the beginning of the 1990s, two noted individuals have reported receiving messages concerning the Mass and the impending crisis it faces. Both of them are considered by many to be authentic, and previous prophecies from their messages have been fulfilled.

In Marmora, Ontario, the Ukrainian visionary, Josyp Terelya, reported that the Virgin Mary told him on August 11, 1993:

Satan shall gain control for a short time over certain parts of the earth, and his rule will extend for forty-two months (Daniel's prophecy of 3 1/2 years). That part of the earth, where Satan shall have full authority over the subjected nations, will experience untold evil and terror as never before. It will be absolutely forbidden to celebrate the holy Sunday, (the Mass) the day of the Resurrection of Christ.[1]

Likewise, in what is probably the most convincing revelation ever given concerning this matter, Fr. Stefano Gobbi reported receiving a detailed message from the Virgin Mary on December 31, 1992.

Our Lady told Fr. Gobbi that the Sacrifice of the Mass would be suppressed and revealed this would be the fulfillment of Daniel's ancient prophecy, a prophecy that says the "daily sacrifice will be abolished for one thousand, two hundred and ninety days."

The message to Fr. Gobbi is titled, "THE END OF TIMES," and as with all the messages he receives, it has an imprimatur from Bishop Donald W. Montrose, D.D. of California and his Eminence Bernardino Cardinal Echeverria Ruiz, O.F.M. of Ecuador. The following is the text of the message given to Fr. Gobbi, reprinted with permission from the Marian Movement of Priests:

> With docility, allow yourselves to be taught by me, beloved children. On this last night of the year, gather together in prayer and in listening to the word of your heavenly Mother, the Prophetess of these last times.
>
> Do not spend these hours noisily or in dissipation, but in silence, in recollection and in contemplation.
>
> I have announced to you many times that the end of the times and the coming of Jesus in glory is very near. Now, I want to help you understand the signs described

in the Holy Scriptures, which indicate that His glorious return is now close.

These signs are clearly indicated in the Gospels, in the letters of Saint Peter and Saint Paul, and they are becoming a reality during these years.

The first sign is the spread of errors, which lead to the loss of faith and to apostasy.

These errors are being propagated by false teachers, by renowned theologians who are no longer teaching the truths of the Gospel, but pernicious heresies based on errors and on human reasoning. It is because of the teaching of these errors that the true faith is being lost and that the Great Apostasy is spreading everywhere.

"See that no one deceives you, for many will attempt to deceive many people. False prophets will come and will deceive very many." (Mt 24:4f5).

"The day of the Lord will not come unless the Great Apostasy comes first." (2 Th 2:3).

"There will be false teachers among you. These will seek to introduce disastrous heresies and will even set themselves against the Master who ransomed them. Many will listen to them and will follow their licentious ways. Through their offense, the Christian faith will be reviled. In their greed, they will exploit you with fabrications." (2 Pet 2:1-3)

The second sign is the outbreak of wars and fratricidal struggles, which lead to the prevalence of violence and hatred and a general slackening off of charity, while natural catastrophes, such as epidemics, famines, floods and earthquakes, become more and more frequent.

"When you hear of reports of wars, close at hand or far away, see that you are not alarmed; for these things must happen. Nation will rise against nation, and kingdom against kingdom. There will be famines and earthquakes in many places. All this will be only the beginning of greater sufferings to come. Evil-doing will be so widespread that the love of many will grow cold. But God will save those who persevere until the end." (Mt 24:6-8, 12-13).

The third sign is the bloody persecution of those who remain faithful to Jesus and to his Gospel and who stand fast in the true faith. Throughout this all, the Gospel will be preached in every part of the world.

Think, beloved children, of the great persecutions to which the Church is being subjected; think of the apostolic zeal of the recent popes, above all of my Pope, John Paul II, as he brings to all the nations of the earth the announcement of the Gospel.

"They will hand you over to persecution, and they will kill you. You will be hated by all because of me. And then many will abandon the faith; they will betray and hate one another. Meanwhile, the message of the kingdom of God will be preached in all the world; all nations must hear it. And then the end will come." (Mt 24:9-10, 14).

The fourth sign is the horrible sacrilege, perpetrated by him who sets himself against Christ, that is, the Antichrist. He will enter into the holy temple of God and will sit on his throne, and have himself adored as God.

"This one will oppose and exalt himself against everything that men adore and call God. The lawless one will come by the power of Satan, with all the force of false miracles and pretended wonders. He will make use of every kind of wicked deception, in order to work harm." (2 Th 2:4,9)

"One day, you will see in the holy place he who commits the horrible sacrilege. The prophet Daniel spoke of this. Let the reader seek to understand." (Mt 24, 15)

BELOVED CHILDREN, IN ORDER TO UNDERSTAND IN WHAT THIS HORRIBLE SACRILEGE CONSISTS, READ WHAT HAS BEEN PREDICTED BY THE PROPHET DANIEL: "GO, DANIEL, THESE WORDS ARE TO REMAIN SECRET AND SEALED UNTIL THE END TIME. MANY WILL BE CLEANSED, MADE WHITE AND UPRIGHT, BUT THE WICKED WILL PERSIST IN DOING WRONG. NOT ONE OF THE WICKED WILL UNDERSTAND THESE THINGS, BUT THE WISE WILL COMPREHEND. NOW, FROM THE MOMENT THAT THE DAILY SACRIFICE IS ABOLISHED AND THE HORRIBLE ABOMINATION IS SET UP, THERE SHALL BE ONE THOUSAND, TWO HUNDRED AND NINETY DAYS. BLESSED IS HE WHO WAITS WITH PATIENCE AND ATTAINS ONE THOUSAND, THREE HUNDRED AND THIRTY-FIVE DAYS." (Dan 12:9-12)

THE HOLY MASS IS THE DAILY SACRIFICE, THE PURE OBLATION WHICH IS OFFERED TO THE LORD EVERYWHERE, FROM THE RISING OF THE SUN TO ITS GOING DOWN.

THE SACRIFICE OF THE MASS RENEWS THAT WHICH WAS ACCOMPLISHED BY JESUS ON CALVARY. BY ACCEPTING THE PROTESTANT DOCTRINE, PEOPLE WILL HOLD THAT THE MASS IS NOT A SACRIFICE BUT ONLY A SACRED MEAL, THAT IS TO SAY, A REMEMBRANCE OF THAT WHICH JESUS DID AT HIS LAST SUPPER. AND THUS, THE CELEBRATION OF HOLY MASS WILL BE SUPPRESSED. IN THIS ABOLITION OF THE DAILY SACRIFICE CONSISTS THE HORRIBLE SACRILEGE ACCOMPLISHED BY THE ANTICHRIST, WHICH WILL LAST ABOUT THREE AND A HALF YEARS, NAMELY, ONE THOUSAND, TWO HUNDRED AND NINETY DAYS.

The fifth sign consists in extraordinary phenomena, which occur in the skies.

"The sun will be darkened, and the moon will not give its light; and the stars will fall from the sky; and the powers of the Heavens will be shaken." (Mt 24:29)

The miracle of the sun, which took place at Fatima during my last apparition, is intended to point out to you that you are now entering into the times when these events will take place, events which will prepare for the return of Jesus in glory.

"And then the sign of the Son of Man will appear in Heaven. All the tribes of the earth will mourn, and men will see the Son of Man coming upon the clouds of Heaven, with great power and splendor." (Mt 24:30)

My beloved ones and children consecrated to my Immaculate Heart, I have wanted to teach you about these signs, which Jesus has pointed out to you in his Gospel, in order to prepare you for the end of the times because these are about to take place in your days.

The year which is coming to a close and that which is beginning form part of the great tribulation, during which the apostasy is spreading, the wars are multiplying, natural catastrophes are occurring in many places, persecutions are intensifying, the announcement of the Gospel is being brought to all nations, extraordinary phenomena are occurring in the sky, and the moment of the full manifestation of the Antichrist is drawing ever nearer.

And so I urge you to remain strong in the faith, secure in trust and ardent in charity. Allow yourselves to be led by me and gather together, each and all, in the sure refuge of my Immaculate Heart, which I have prepared for you especially during these last times. Read, with me, the signs of your time, and live in peace of heart and in confidence.

I am always with you, to tell you that the coming about of these signs indicates to you with certainty that the end of the times with the return of Jesus in glory, is close at hand.

"Learn a lesson from the fig tree: When its branches become tender and sprout the first leaves, you know that summer is near. In the same way, when you see these things taking place, know that your liberation is near." (Mt 24: 32-33).[2]

A little more that two years later, on March 11, 1995, Mary again spoke to Fr. Gobbi about the approaching fulfillment of Daniel's words. Here is that entire message, entitled "MY SECRET:"

In this, my venerated shrine, I welcome you all, my beloved ones and children consecrated to me, that I may enclose you all within the safe refuge of my Immaculate Heart.

Here, I appeared as the woman clothed in the sun, to point out to you the road along which you must journey in this century of yours, so ensnared and in the possession of the Spirit of Evil.

Here, I came from Heaven to offer you the refuge in which to take shelter at the moment of the great struggle between me and my adversary, and in the painful hours of the great tribulation and chastisement.

Here, I caused the Marian Movement of Priests to spring up and, by means of this little son whom I have brought to every part of the world during these years, I have formed for myself the cohort, now ready for the battle and for my greatest victory.

I want you here today, spiritually united with this son of mine, as a great cenacle of my Movement is being held before the image of your heavenly Mother placed in the very spot where I appeared to the three children, Jacinta, Francisco and Lucia.

Here, I am gathering you all around about me and expressing to you my pleasure for the way in which you have accepted the invitation to become part of the Marian Movement of Priests, to consecrate yourselves to my Immaculate Heart and to spread everywhere cenacles of prayer among priests, children, youth and families.

I want you spiritually here with me, because as of now you are entering into the last period of time of this century of yours, when the events which I have predicted to you will come to their complete fulfillment. For this reason, here in the very place where I appeared, I want today to reveal to you my secret.

In the Church, the Great Apostasy, which will spread throughout the whole world, will be brought to its completion; the schism will take place through a general alienation from the Gospel and from the true faith. THERE WILL ENTER INTO THE CHURCH A MAN OF INIQUITY, WHO OPPOSES HIMSELF TO CHRIST, AND WHO WILL BRING INTO HER INTERIOR THE ABOMINATION OF DESOLATION, THUS BRINGING TO FULFILLMENT THE HORRIBLE SACRILEGE, OF WHICH THE PROPHET DANIEL HAS SPOKEN. (MT 24, 15)

My secret concerns humanity.

Humanity will reach the summit of corruption and impiety, of rebellion against God and of open opposition to His law of love. It will know the hour of its greatest chastisement, which has already been foretold to you by the prophet Zechariah. (Zech 13,7-9)

Then this place will appear to all as a bright sign of my motherly presence, in the supreme hour of your great tribulation. From here, my light will spread to every part of the world and from this fount will gush the water of Divine Mercy, which will descend to irrigate the barrenness of a world, now reduced to an immense desert.

And in this, my extraordinary work of love and salvation, there will appear to all the triumph of the Immaculate Heart of her who is invoked as Mother of Mercy.[2]

These messages from the Virgin Mary to Josyp Terelya and Fr. Gobbi give us an insight into God's warnings over the centuries about the importance of the mysteries of the faith. These warnings have also come through many Eucharistic signs and revelations that point to Christ's True Presence in the Eucharist and the Sacrifice of the Mass.

But Mary's revelations to these visionaries are also accompanied by a myriad of questions, such as: Who will this individual be, a religious or a political figure? How will he be able to accomplish this horrible action? And will there be, as some suspect, a false pope and a schism in the Church?

No one knows for sure; however, one thing is certain: The Virgin's revelations concerning this danger are not to be taken lightly. Furthermore, a closer look at what Church Fathers and Doctors have said will help us better understand this mystery.

CHAPTER FOUR

THE EUCHARIST:
A LINE OF DEMARCATION

The Second Vatican Council's Dogmatic Constitution on Divine Revelation detailed the method by which revelation is handed down and established that the principal intention of the Old Testament was to show that the Old Covenant was a preparation for the coming of Christ, the Redeemer of all. These books help us know God and His plan of salvation.

Most importantly, the Dogmatic Constitution defined how the books of the Old Testament reveal their full meaning in the New Testament.

The Council wrote:

> God, the inspirer and author of both Testaments, wisely arranged that the New Testament be hidden in the Old, and the Old be made manifest in the New. For, though Christ established the New Covenant in His blood (see Lk 22:20; 1 Cor 11:25), still the books of the Old Testament with all their parts, caught up in the proclamation of the Gospel, acquire and show forth their full meaning in the New Testament (see Mt 5:17; Lk 24:27; Rom 16:25-26; 2 Cor 3: 14-16) and in turn shed light on it and explain it.

Indeed, as Christ told two travelers on the road to Emmaus, His life and death fulfilled the words of the prophets. Christ said, "How slow you are to believe all that the prophets have announced." (Lk 24:25) Afterwards, when Christ appeared again, this time to all the apostles, He told them, "Recall those words I spoke to you when I was still with you, that everything written about Me in the law of Moses, and Psalms had to be fulfilled." (Lk 24:44) Scripture then says Christ "opened their minds to the understanding of the Scriptures." (Lk 24: 45) Therefore, no Christian can ignore how the words of the Old Testament are fulfilled in the events of the New.

Likewise, even though the mystery of salvation is fulfilled with the completion of Divine Revelation, Christ, in His own words, foretells that which must occur before the end of the world, and His words again relate to the Old Testament prophets.

Most significantly , the Lord specifically states that the prophecy of Daniel will be fulfilled at a future time. In fact, he refers to no other Old Testament prophet when He foretells the future:

"When you see the abominable and destructive thing which the prophet Daniel foretold standing on holy ground (let the reader take note!), those in Judea must flee to the mountains." (Mt 24:15)

Scripture tells us that during their lifetime, the apostles and disciples continued to place credence in Christ's admonition about how events would unfold and His words would be fulfilled. They especially kept in mind Daniel's prophecies, just as Christ advised them to. In his Letter to the Thessalonians (2 Th 2:3-4, 8-9), some scholars say St. Paul parallels the writings of the Book of Daniel as does St. John in his first epistle (1 Jn 2:18-23).

Moreover, many scholars believe that St. John's Book of Revelation cannot be properly interpreted without knowledge of the Book of Daniel. The symbolism common to both books, such as horns and beasts, is apparent.

Indeed, over the centuries, many writers have cross-referenced these books, searching for clues to support their interpretations of the end times, which will reportedly "fulfill" the prophecies they contain.

The Gospels and the Book of Revelation, as well as the Book of Daniel, presuppose the future of the world has been decided. God will rise up to overthrow the powers of the world and then rule forever. These books also emphasize that God exercises divine control over the historic events that will ultimately lead to this triumph. Experts tell us Christ is the central figure who guides believers toward the promised kingdom. While Christ's role is apparent in the books of the New Testament, He is portrayed as the mysterious figure whose "dominion is an everlasting dominion" in Chapter 7 of the Book of Daniel.

Theologians say that specific verses in Daniel also foretell Christ as the coming Messiah, which is confirmed by the use of the term "Son of Man," found in Daniel, the four Gospels and the Book of Revelation.

In the Book of Daniel, we read, "One like the Son of Man coming on the clouds of Heaven." (Dan 7:13)

Similarly, in Matthew, Jesus calls Himself the Son of Man: "To help you realize the Son of Man has authority on earth to forgive sins..." (Mt 9:6)

"When the Son of Man comes in his glory, escorted by all the angels of Heaven, he will sit upon his Royal Throne." (Mt 25:31)

"Who do they say the Son of Man is?" (Mt 16:13)

"After that, men will see the Son of Man coming on a cloud with great power and glory." (Lk 21:27)

Finally, in the Book of Revelation we read, "One like the Son of Man wearing an ankle-length robe, with a sash of gold about his breast." (Rev 1:13) and "Then, as I watched, a white cloud appeared, and on the cloud sat one like a Son of Man ..." (Rev. 14:14)

Biblical scholars have often cited these verses to demonstrate the correlation of events in the New Testament with events in the Old. But even more significantly, these verses directly link Daniel's visions and words with Christ's life and words.

Thus, just as Daniel ties his prophecies to Christ, so too Christ (Mt 24:15) makes it clear that the meaning of some His prophecies are to be found in Daniel.

Since Christ's words in Matthew 24:15 pertain to a period after His earthly life, the Fathers believed this prophecy's fulfillment was related to the Church, Christ's Mystical Body on earth, and especially to liturgical worship. According to scholars, St. Paul's and St. John's letters convey the same meaning.

Theologian Vincent P. Miceli, S.J., in his book, *The Antichrist*, explains how the early Church viewed this scenario. Writes Fr. Miceli:

> The Fathers of the Church emphasize the corruption of the liturgy that will prevail in the last days. As the end draws near, the Church will be subjected to a fiercer, more diabolical persecution than any previously suffered. There will be a cessation of all religious worship. They will take away the Sacrifice.[1]

Indeed, this teaching about a formidable assault by the Antichrist on the Church's sacred mysteries has existed over the centuries. The Greek Fathers, who were directly associated with the apostles, wrote with great authority on this issue. Both St. Irenaeus (A.D. 135) and St. Cyril (A.D. 315) of Jerusalem refer to Daniel's visions when interpreting Christ's prophetic words. In addition, saints Clement of Alexandria, Athanasius, Basil the Great, Gregory of Nyssa, Gregory of Nazianzus, and John Chrysostom all upheld the traditional teachings on this matter.

St. Hippolytus, who lived during the 1st century, wrote that the Antichrist will order the destruction of all things that remind men of Jesus Christ and will prohibit under penalty of death, the administering of the sacraments and the offering of the Holy Sacrifice of the Mass. Hippolytus also wrote that the Mass would have to be celebrated in forests and secret places, just as it was in the early Church.

The Latin Fathers, too, referred to Daniel's prophecies in their writings about the future trials of the Church. St. Augustine cited Daniel and said that "whoever reads portions of Daniel even half-asleep" cannot fail to see that the Church will be greatly assailed; this same interpretation is found in early writings dealing with the "end times."

Many medieval writers wrote in depth about the terrifying theme of the Apocalypse. Like the early Fathers, they were motivated by predictions that the end to the world was at hand. Their works centered around the early Fathers' writings and Scripture, and emphasized the signs that will accompany the rise of the Antichrist, especially as presented in the Book of Daniel and discerned from Matthew's Gospel and the Book of Revelation.

St. Robert Bellarmine, who died in 1621 and was the last Doctor of the Church to specialize in the study of eschatology, wrote:

> For it must be known that in the divine letters (Scripture), the Holy Spirit to have given to us six sure signs concerning the coming of Antichrist: two of which precede the Antichrist himself, namely the preaching of

the Gospel in the whole world, and the devastation of the Roman Empire: the two contemporaneous men (the Two Witnesses), which it is to be seen prophesied, Enoch and Elias, and the greatest and last persecution, and also that the PUBLIC SACRIFICE (of the Mass) SHALL COMPLETELY CEASE, the two following (signs) surely, the death of Antichrist after three and a half years (after his rise to power) and the end of the world: none of which signs we have seen at this time.[2]

Desmond H. Birch, in his extensive study of writings about the end times, which progresses to and includes St. Robert Bellarmine, provides this summation of his findings concerning the Antichrist and the traditional interpretation of Daniel's prophetic words:

> Scripture itself speaks of the "abomination of desolations" during which the perpetual "Sacrifice" (the Sacrifice of the Eucharistic liturgy) shall cease. Antichrist shall have outlawed the saying of Mass. Many prophecies state that during this period, the Mass will only be said in the "desert" (wilderness). The Christians will have fled the cities which are controlled by Antichrist. Certain priests will have gone into the wilderness to serve the Christians in hiding. *(Trial, Tribulation and Triumph,* Queenship Publishing, 1996)[3]

From the 19th century to the modern era, more scholarly writings are found concerning the end times and the fulfillment of Daniel's words. As in the writings of the Fathers and medieval Doctors, the focus continued to be on the appearance of an Antichrist, who it is generally accepted will assail the Church and, according to some, all religion. An examination of one writer gives us insight into the thinking of this era concerning the fulfillment of this prophecy.

John Henry Newman (1801-1890), a Catholic convert and acknowledged scholar, wrote with authority on this topic. Cardinal

Newman foresaw the total loss of the Church's temporal power, and he saw signs that Daniel's prophecies were moving toward fulfillment in 19th century society.

He was convinced that the Great Apostasy against the Church was beginning, and he recognized parallels between the Jews, who repeatedly fell away from their faith, and the various heresies that the Catholic Church confronted over the centuries, from Arianism to the Age of Enlightenment. Cardinal Newman related the errors of each generation to his own times and envisioned a climate that would eventually favor the rise of the Antichrist.

It was in the "peaceful civilized nations" that Cardinal Newman anticipated the greatest danger because he recognized a determined effort toward government without religion. He saw this as attempting "to rule without truth."

Cardinal Newman realized that many countries were striving to remove all religion from public activities, such as education, the press and political affairs. "Utility" would be the principle on which social interaction would be based, not the principle of Truth.

In the end, Cardinal Newman saw that the objective validity of religion would be denied, as would its historical reality. Rather, personal feelings, experiences and psychological formation would take precedence. - which is exactly what has occurred.

He also cited what he believed to be the principal cause of this crisis. It was the "Evil One," who was bringing about the apostasy. Cardinal Newman wrote:

> He (Satan) offers baits to tempt men; he promises liberty, equality, trade and wealth, remission of taxes, reforms. He tempts men to rail against their rulers and superiors in imitation of his own revolution. He promises illumination,

knowledge, science, philosophy, enlargement of mind. He scoffs at times gone by; at saved traditions, at every institution which reveres them. He bids man mount aloft, to become God. He laughs and jokes with men, gets intimate with them, takes their hands, gets his fingers between theirs, grasps them and then they are his.[4]

Cardinal Newman's perceptions are uncanny in their accuracy, and today's world reflects the crisis he predicted.

Most frightening of all, in words that foreshadow the fulfillment of Daniel's prophecy, Cardinal Newman wrote that in the final trials of the Church, "They shall take away the daily sacrifice."

In about the same period, a mystic and stigmatist, who lived for years only on the Eucharist, echoed Cardinal Newman's perceptions of the coming trial in one of her prophecies.

The Venerable Anne Catherine Emmerich (1774-1824), an Augustinian nun from Westphalia, Germany, received a powerful vision that showed her the Mass was the line of demarcation between men in both time and eternity and that at a particular moment in history, "the Holy Sacrifice of the Mass would cease." She also saw that the Church would triumph around the year 2000.

Sadly, many modern writers fear they will lose their credibility if they speak openly about the existence of Satan and his efforts to topple the Church and its sacred mysteries; nevertheless, there are some who echo Cardinal Newman's words.

Like Desmond Birch, and Fr. Miceli, Fr. Randall Paine, ORC in his book, *His Time Is Short: The Devil and His Agenda* (Imprimatur: Archbishop John R. Roach of St. Paul and Minneapolis), concurs that in our time Satan is forging ahead with his plan to discredit the dogma of Christ's True Presence in the Eucharist and to end the Holy

Sacrifice of the Mass — just as Mary has been warning us in her revelations.

Writes Father Paine:

> Satan's sifting will be nowhere so thorough as there where the wheat of the earth has quite literally been lifted to the Cross of Christ. I mean the Eucharist. The Church grew slowly to recognize the full riches the Lord has laid into this mystery, and soon the Sacrifice of the Mass became the central act in the construction of the Heavenly Jerusalem. But Satan came to recognize this too. And he has been working overtime in the last 30 years to find ways to bring the whole, awe-inspiring structure of the Church's liturgy to a ludicrous collapse.[5]

CHAPTER FIVE

"THE SACRIFICE WILL NEVER CEASE"

Shortly before Venerable Anne Catherine Emmerich and John Henry Cardinal Newman, another great figure in the Church wrote about Daniel's prophecy and how it relates to the Holy Sacrifice of the Mass.

St. Alphonsus Liguori (1696-1787) was the founder of the Redemptorists order and was renowned for preaching missions and hearing confessions. The author of many books, St. Alphonsus was canonized in 1839, and Pope Pius IX declared him a Doctor of the Church in 1871. In 1950, Pope Pius XII declared him the patron of moral theologians and confessors.

A theologian with great insights into the Eucharist, St. Alphonsus wrote extensively on the sacrificial aspects of the Mass and how it fulfilled the Old and New Testaments.

Most significantly, St. Alphonsus believed the meaning of Daniel's prophecy applied specifically to the Sacrifice of the Mass. He wrote:

> This offering which our Lord made then did not limit itself to that moment. It began then; it has continued since; it will continue forever. It will cease on earth only at the time of the Antichrist, as Daniel foretold (Dan 12: 11).[1]

In another one of his writings, St. Alphonsus elaborated on Daniel's reference of the "abolishment of the sacrifice."

"The devil has always managed to get rid of the Mass by means of the heretics," he said, "making them the precursors of the Antichrist who, above all else, will manage to abolish, and in fact will succeed in abolishing, as a punishment for the sins of men, the Holy Sacrifice of the Altar, precisely as Daniel had predicted." (St. Alphonsus Liguori, "La Messa e l'Officio Strapazzati" in Opere Ascetiche)[2]

The writings of St. Alphonsus Liguori, along with previously quoted authorities and the Virgin Mary's revelations to Fr. Stefano Gobbi and other contemporary visionaries, are significant in three ways.

First, these revelations call upon Christians and especially Catholics, to discern the truth about what appear to be conflicting interpretations of Daniel's prophecy. Many Protestant ministers continue to preach that Daniel's prophecy concerning "the abolishment of the sacrifice" deals not with the Sacrifice of the Mass, but with the eventual reinstitution of the daily sacrifice of animals by the Jews in the Temple on the Mount in Jerusalem. This would then be followed, in their opinion, by a cessation of the Jews' renewed sacrifices for 42 months, thus fulfilling Daniel's words.

Some televangelical ministers have even traveled to Jerusalem to interview orthodox Jews who hold elaborate plans to rebuild the temple on the Mount, where a Moslem mosque of great significance to the Islamic faith now sits. These Jewish fundamentalists say they wish to reinstitute the sacrifices of their forefathers, which they believe will then fulfill Scripture. They also claim that this will lead them to find the true Messiah.

Even though some historically important events dealing with the Jewish people, Jerusalem and the Antichrist must still occur,

Church tradition is clear that the true meaning of Daniel's warning about the "abolishment of the Sacrifice" refers to the Mass.

The second important element to understand is that the Mass, which is the perpetual renewal of Christ's death on the cross, is the true and perfect sacrifice that fulfills Old Testament prophecies.

St. Alphonsus Liguori explains this relationship:

> The Sacrifice of our Lord was a perfect sacrifice of which those sacrifices of the Old Law were but signs, figures and what the apostle calls "weak and destitute elemental powers." (Gal 4:9) The Sacrifice offered by Jesus Christ really fulfilled all the conditions mentioned above.
>
> The first condition, sanctification, or the consecration of the victim, was accomplished in the Incarnation of the Word by God the Father, Himself, as St. John reports, "the one whom the Father has consecrated" (Jn 10:36). When the Archangel Gabriel announced to the Blessed Virgin that she was chosen to be the Mother of the Son of God, he said, "The child to be born will be called holy, the Son of God." (Lk 1:35)
>
> This divine victim, who was to be sacrificed for the salvation of the world, had already been sanctified by God when he was born of Mary. From the first moment in which the Eternal Word took a human body, he was consecrated to God to be the victim of the great sacrifice that was to be accomplished on the Cross for the salvation of mankind. Therefore Christ said to the Father, "But a body you prepared for me ... I come to do Your Will, O God." (Heb 10:5, 7).
>
> The second condition, the oblation or offering, was also fulfilled at the moment of the Incarnation when Jesus Christ voluntarily offered himself to atone for the

sins of mankind. Knowing that divine justice could not be satisfied by all the ancient sacrifices, nor by all the works of mankind, he offered himself to atone for all sins and said to God: "Sacrifice and offering you did not desire ... holocausts and sin offerings you took no delight in. Then I said, 'Behold I come to do Your Will.'" (Heb 10:5-7)

Then St. Paul adds, "By this 'will' we will have been consecrated through the offering of the body of Jesus Christ once for all." (Heb 10:10) This text is indeed remarkable. Sin had rendered mankind unworthy of being offered to God and of being accepted by Him; therefore it was necessary that Jesus Christ should offer Himself for us in order to sanctify us by His grace and to make us worthy of being accepted by God.

The third condition of sacrifice — the immolation of the victim — was obviously accomplished by the death of our Lord on the Cross.

Finally, we must look at the consumption and partaking which complete a perfect sacrifice. The consumption is accomplished by the Resurrection, when Christ shed all that was terrestrial and mortal and was clothed in divine glory. He had asked His Father to glorify Him (Jn 17:5), but it was not the divine glory which He possessed from all eternity. It was for His humanity that He prayed.

The partaking in the perfect sacrifice was accomplished in Heaven where all the blessed are partakers of the victim's triumph.

The two conditions of consumption and communion are manifestly fulfilled in the Sacrifice of the Altar, which, as the Council of Trent declared, is the same as that of the Cross. In fact, the Sacrifice of the Mass instituted by our Lord before his death, is a continuation of the Sacrifice of the Cross.

Jesus Christ wished that the price of His blood, shed for the salvation of mankind, should be applied to us by the Sacrifice of the Altar. In it, the victim offered is the same, though present there in an unbloody manner. Thus said the Council of Trent:

"Although Christ our Lord was to offer Himself once to His Eternal Father on the altar of the Cross by actually dying to obtain for us eternal redemption, yet as His priesthood was not to become extinct by His death, in order to leave His Church a visible sacrifice suited to the present condition of mankind, a sacrifice which might at the same time represent to us the bloody sacrifice consummated on the Cross, preserve the memory of it to the end of the world and apply the salutary fruits of it for the remission of the sin we daily commit ...

"At His last supper, on the very night on which He was betrayed, giving proof that He was established a priest forever according to the order of Melchizedek, he offered to God the Father His body and blood, under the appearances of bread and wine, and, under the same symbols, gave them to the apostles, whom He constituted at the same time priests of the New Law.

"By these words, 'Do this in remembrance of me,' He commissioned them and their successors in the priesthood to consecrate and offer His body and blood, as the Catholic Church has always understood and taught (Sess. 22, c.1)."

In the very next chapter, the Council declares that the Lord, appeased by the oblation of the Sacrifice of the Mass, grants us His graces and the remission of sins. "It is one and the same victim; the one that offers sacrifice is the same one who, after having sacrificed Himself on the Cross, offers Himself now by the ministry of the priest;

there is no difference except in the manner of offering (Sess. 22, c.2)[3]"

Besides St. Alphonsus' explanation of the validity of the perpetual Sacrifice of the Holy Mass, scholars note that Scripture also foretold the ceasing of the bloody animal sacrifices. For example, in the book of Hosea, we read:

> "For the children of Israel shall sit many days without a king, and without price, and without sacrifice, and without altar, and without ephod, and without teraphim; and after this the children of Israel will return and shall seek the Lord their God and David their king; and they shall fear the Lord and His goodness in the last days."

In his writings, St. Alphonsus also stated that abolishing the sacrifice would not be complete and that the "true Sacrifice" would always continue as there would always be the offering of the Mass.

Indeed, contemporary visionaries also emphasize that the Mass will always continue to be offered; however, much like the early apostles and disciples were forced to conceal their services of worship, it is prophesied that at some point the true offering of the Mass may have to be held clandestinely or apart from what will be considered the mainstream practice of the faith. While all this seems mysterious, St. Alphonsus again offers some clarification:

> The sacrifice of Jesus Christ will never cease since the Son of God will always continue to offer Himself to His Father by an eternal sacrifice, for He Himself is the priest and the victim, not according to the order of Aaron of which the priesthood and the sacrifice were temporary, imperfect and inadequate to appease the anger of God against rebellious mankind, but according to the order of

Melchizedek, as David predicted: "You are a priest forever according to the order of Melchizedek." (Ps 110:4)

The priesthood of Jesus Christ will be eternal, since even after the end of this world, He will always continue to offer in Heaven this same victim that He once offered on the Cross for the glory of God and for the salvation of mankind.[4]

How and when the cessation or suppression of the Mass will occur, perhaps because of a shift in Church teachings or legislated by a political action, is unclear. But this much is certain: even with the fulfillment of this prophecy, nothing can occur that would conflict with the promises in Scripture. This is understood to refer specifically to Christ's words to Peter: "I for my part declare to you, you are 'Rock' and on this rock, I will build my Church, and the jaws of death will not prevail against it" (Mt 16:18), and to Christ's words at the end of Matthew's Gospel, "And know that I am with you always, until the end of the world." (Mt 28:20)

With these verses, theologians see an implicit guarantee that Christ's True Presence will remain until the end of the world despite the references to an "abolition."

The third element of Daniel's prophecy involves the faithful's need to heed the warning. Believers must be vigilant and prepared so that through prayer, reparation and public action they can respond to any activity that threatens the Church's sacred mysteries.

As noted, while a total abolition of the Holy Sacrifice of the Mass is generally viewed as impossible, we must not underestimate what could possibly occur to suppress the Mass. Indeed, it would not be such a heralded prophecy if anything less than a widespread impact occurs. Thus, to whatever degree this prophecy may someday be fulfilled, and regardless of when, it will probably produce an unprecedented effect on the world.

Today more than 350,000 Masses are offered each day. This continual offering of the bloodless sacrifice spiritually fortifies the world to endure the perils and consequences of sin that plague humanity, according to saints, popes and mystics. Withdrawing this grace would have pervasive negative effect on the harmonious function of the world. The extent of the damage cannot be estimated since there is no way of measuring the mystical equation of grace that sustains our world.

Fr. P. Huchede, a highly respected 19th century professor of theology at the Grand Seminary of Laval, France, wrote a timeless work titled, *History of the Antichrist*, which postulates what could occur if the Holy Mass were altered or interrupted; he also concurs with St. Alphonsus and others about the nature of Daniel's prophecy.

His work was first published in 1884, which is believed to be the year Pope Leo XIII had his famous vision of Satan's confrontation with God. Fr. Huchede wrote:

> No language can give an adequate idea of the atrocity and effects of this frightful persecution. "I beheld and, lo, that horn made war against the saints, and prevailed over them." (Dan 7:21) "The beast shall make war against the saints, and shall overcome them and kill them." (Rev 11:7) And he "shall crush the saints of the Most High." (Dan 7: 25) "And he will put to death all those who will not adore the image of the beast." (Rev 13:15) Then shall the truth be oppressed. The Church shall see her children apostatize in vast numbers, and in the agony of her heartrending grief, she will cry out in the words of her divine spouse, "My God, My God, why hast thou forsaken me?" (Mk 15:34)

"THEN BY ORDER OF THE TYRANT, THE CONTINUAL SACRIFICE SHALL BE ABOLISHED." (Dan 9:27) THE HOLY SACRIFICE OF THE MASS SHALL NO LONGER BE OFFERED UP PUBLICLY ON THE ALTARS. The Church shall be devastated; the sacred vessels desecrated; the priests shall be scattered and separated from their flocks and be put to death. The beauty of the new Zion has vanished! Her priests sigh; her streets resound with wailings and lamentations because there is no one found to assist at the solemnities of the Lamb. The Church has taken up her abode in the catacombs. (Jerem. Thren-Lamentations)

All the faithful shall be terror-stricken, for there is nothing to equal the ferocity with which the beast will persecute the Church. "The beast which I saw," says St. John, "was like to a leopard, and his feet were as the feet of a bear, and his mouth as the mouth of a lion." (Rev 13: 2) Those who will refuse him obedience, says St. Gregory (32 Moral., c. 12), shall perish in the midst of the most excruciating torments. They shall be tortured by infernal engines of pain such as had never been thought of before. The persecutors will add to the terror of punishment the prestige of miracles, which makes St. Gregory exclaim in a state of bewilderment, "What a frightful temptation for the human heart! Behold a martyr who delivers over his body to torture, and his executioner performs miracles before his eyes!" Where is the virtue that would not receive a profound shock in the presence of such a scene? "Woe, then, to land and sea because the devil is come down unto you having great wrath, knowing that he hath but a short time." (Rev 12:12) "And a time shall come such as never was from the time that nations began even until that time." (Mt 24:21; Mk 13:19)[5]

Thus, based on Fr. Huchede's interpretation of the prophesied trials of the Church and messages of contemporary visionaries, Daniel's words concerning an "abolishment" are exactly what the faithful need to focus on.

Scripture and theologians have made it clear the Antichrist's identity will remain a secret until he finally appears. Afterward, his reign will be painful, but short and futile. Before he comes, however, the little flock of the Remnant Church must be prepared. They must recognize the Antichrist by his "actions," especially any action that "affects" the Sacrifice of the Mass or its validity.

Indeed, the fulfillment of Daniel's prophecy promises to be a significant moment in salvation history. Let us, therefore, adhere to the to the words of our dear Savior in Scripture who said, **"Be vigilant at all times and pray that you have the strength to escape tribulations that are imminent and to stand before the Son of Man"**. (Lk 21:36)

NOTES

Introduction -

1. Desmond A. Birch, *Trial, Tribulation & Triumph* (Santa Barbara, California: Queenship Publishing Company 1996), p. 509

Chapter Three -

1. Josyp Terelya, *In The Kingdom of the Spirit*, (Abba House, Pueblo, Colorado: 1995), pp. 86-87

2. Stefano Gobbi, *To The Priest, Our Lady's Beloved Sons*, (Marian Movement of Priests, St. Francis, Maine) pp. 801-804

Chapter Four -

1. Vincent P. Miceli, S.J., *The Anitchrist* (Harrison, New York: Roman Catholic Books, 1981), p. 202

2. Op. Cit. *Trial, Tribulations and Triumph*, p. 475

3. Ibid p. 475

4. Op. Cit. *The Antichrist.* pp.102-125

5. Rev. Randall Pain, ORC *His Time His Short: The Devil and His Agenda* (Saint Paul Minnesota: The Leaflet Missal Company, 1989), p. 96

Chapter Five -

1. St. Alphonsus Liguori, *The Holy Eucharist* (Staten Island, New York: Alba House, 1994), p. 7

2. Op. Cit. *The Antichrist*, p. 276

3. Liguori, Op. Cit. p. 6

4. Ibid. p. 7

5. Rev. P. Huchede, *History of the Antichrist*, Rockford, Illinois: Tan Books and Publishers, Inc. 1981, p. 35

SELECTED BIBLIOGRAPHY

Alonso, J.M. and B. Billet, B. Borinskoy, R. Laurentin. *True and False Apparitions in the Church* (2nd Ed.). St. Laurent Montreal: Editions, Belarmine. (no date).

Birch, Desmond. *Trial Tribulation and Triumph*. Santa Barbara, California: Queenship Publishing Company, 1996.

Bunson, Matthew. *Encyclopedia of Catholic History.* Huntington, Indiana: Our Sunday Visitor, Inc., 1995.

Brown, Rev. Eugene M. (ed.) *Dreams, Visions & Prophecies of Don Bosco.* New Rochelle, New York: Don Bosco Publications, 1986.

———. *Catechism of the Catholic Church.* (English Translation): United States Catholic Conference, Inc., 1994.

Carroll, Rev. Msgr. Richard L. *The Remnant Church*. Chelsea, Michigan: Book Crafters, 1993.

Carroll, Rev. Msgr. Richard L. *The Third Millennium The Triumph of Our Lady.* Chelsea, Michigan: Carroll, 1996

Flynn, Ted and Maureen. *The Thunder of Justice*. Sterling, Virginia: MaxKol Communications, Inc., 1993.

Giese, Rev. Vincent. *John Henry Newman Heart to Heart*. New Rochelle, New York: New City Press, 1993.

Gobbi, Don Stefano. *Our Lady Speaks to Her Beloved Priests.* St. Francis, Maine: National Headquarters of the Marian Movement of Priests in the United States of America, 1988.

Huchede, Rev. P. *History of Antichrist.* Rockford, Illinois: TAN Books and Publishers, Inc., 1974.

Kramer, Rev., Herman Bernard. *The Book of Destiny.* Rockford, Illinois: TAN Books and Publishers, Inc., 1955.

Laurentin, Rene. *The Apparitions of the Blessed Virgin Mary Today.* Paris France: Veritas Publications, 1991.

Liguori, St. Alphonsus. *The Holy Eucharist.* Staten Island, New York: Alba House, 1994.

Miceli, Vincent P., S.J. The Antichrist. Harrison, New York: Roman Catholic Books, 1981.

Montague, George T., S.M. *The Apocalypse.* Ann Arbor, Michigan: Servant Publications, 1992.

O'Connor, Fr. Edward, C.S.C. *Marian Apparitions Today Why So Many?* Santa Barabara, California: Queenship Publishing Company, 1996.

Paine, Rev. Randall, ORC. *His Time is Short: The Devil and His Agenda.* Saint Paul, Minnesota: The Leaflet Missal Company, 1989.

Petrisko, Thomas W. *Call of the Ages.* Santa Barbara, California: Queenship Publishing Company, 1995.

Petrisko, Thomas W. (ed.) *Our Lady Queen of Peace* - Special Edition I, Pittsburgh, Pennsylvania: Pittsburgh Center for Peace, Inc., 1991.

Petrisko, Thomas W. *The Sorrow, the Sacrifice, and the Triumph, The Apparitions, Visions and Prophecies of Christina Gallagher.* New York: Simon and Schuster, Inc., 1995.

Schmoger, Very Rev. Carl E., C.SS.R. *The Life of Anne Catherine Emmerich - Volume I*. Rockford, Illinois: TAN Books and Publishers, Inc., 1976.

Schmoger, Very Rev. Carl E., C.SS.R. *The Life of Anne Catherine Emmerich - Volume 2*. Rockford, Illinois: TAN Books and Publishers, Inc., 1976.

Senior, Donald (ed.) *The Catholic Study Bible New American Bible*. New York, New York: Oxford University Press, Inc., 1990

Terelya, Josyp. *In the Kingdom of the Spirit*. Pueblo, Colorado: Abbahouse, 1995.

——. *The Holy Bible Douay Rheims Versio*n. Rockford Illionois: TAN Books and Publishers, Inc.

——. *The New American Bible*. Witchita, Kansas: Catholic Bible Publishers, 1984-85 Edition.

——. *The Universal Standard Encyclopedia*. New York: Standard Reference Works PUblishing Company, Inc., 1956.

Williams, Thomas David. *The Textural Concordance of Holy Scriptures*. Rockford, Illinois: TAN Books and Publishers, Inc., 1985.

Freze, Michael, S.F.O. *The Making of Saints*. Huntington, Indiana: Our Sunday Vistor, Inc., 1991.

THE 'THIRD SECRET OF FATIMA' VISION

Special Edition Prints Available!

Prayer Card	$ 1.00		*Includes Shipping*
8 x 10" Print Only	$ 5.00	+ $2.00	S/H
12 x 16" Print Only	$ 8.00	+ $4.00	S/H

TO ORDER CALL: 1-412-787-9735
PLEASE CALL FOR QUANTITY PURCHASES

Help Spread the 'Queen of Peace' Newspaper!

Secret of Fatima Edition

This 2001 edition takes a closer look at the Secret of Fatima, and in particular, the 'Third Secret' which was revealed by the Church on June 26, 2000. Included is the commentary written by Cardinal Ratzinger, which accompanied the secret's release.

Afterlife Edition

This edition examines the actual places of Heaven, Hell and Purgatory through the eyes of the Saints, Mystics, Visionaries, and Blessed Mother herself. Will you be ready come judgment day?

Illumination Edition

This edition focuses on a coming 'day of enlightenment' in which every person on earth will see their souls in the same light that God sees them. Commonly referred to as the 'Warning' or 'Mini-Judgment', many saints and visionaries, particularly the Blessed Mother have spoken about this great event, now said to be imminent.

Eternal Father Edition

This edition makes visible the love and tenderness of God the Father and introduces a special consecration to Him. Many of His messages for the world today tell of the great love He has for all of His 'Prodigal Children.'

Holy Spirit Edition

This edition reveals how the Holy Spirit continues to work through time and history, raising up great saints in the Church. Emphasized in the hidden, yet important role of Saint Joseph.

Eucharistic Edition

This edition contains evidence for the Real Presence of Christ in the Eucharist. Many miracles and messages are recorded to reaffirm this truth.

Special Edition III

This edition focuses on the great prophecies the Blessed Mother has given to the world since her apparitions in 1917 at Fatima. Prophetic events related to the 'Triumph of Her Immaculate Heart' are addressed in detail.

Special Edition II

This edition examines the apparitions of the Blessed Mother at Fatima and in relation to today's apparitions occurring worldwide.

Special Edition I

The first in a trilogy of the apparitions and messages of the Blessed Mother, this edition tells why Mary has come to earth and is appearing to all parts of the world today.

Best Sellers by Dr. Thomas W. Petrisko!

Inside Heaven and Hell

What History, Theology and Mystics Tell Us About the Afterlife
Take a spiritual journey with the saints, mystics, visionaries, and the
Blessed Mother - inside Heaven and Hell! Discover what really
happens at your judgment. With profound new insight into what
awaits each one of us, this book is a *must read for all those who
are serious about earning their 'salvation.'*   **$ 14.95**

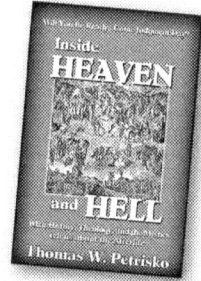

Inside Purgatory

What History, Theology, and the Mystics tell us about Purgatory
The follow up book to the best-seller '*Inside Heaven and Hell*'
this books continues on in the same 'reader-friendly' format.
Guiding the reader through the teachings of the Church
and Scripture, this book is also enhanced by what mystics,
visionaries, saints and scholars tell us about this mysterious
place. **$10.95**

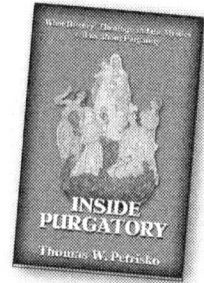

The Miracle of the
Illumination of All Consciences

Known as the 'Warning' or 'Mini-Judgment' a coming "day of
enlightenment" has been foretold. It is purported to be a day
in which God will supernaturally illuminate the conscience
of every man, woman, and child on earth. Each person, then,
would momentarily see the state of their soul through God's
eyes and realize the truth of His existence.   **$12.95**

Fatima's Third Secret Explained

Officially made public to the world on June 26, 2000, the
controversial *Third Secret* of Fatima is not easily understood.
This work seeks to explain the *Third Secret* in the context of the
entire message of Fatima and decipher what it might mean for
the world today. Included is the invaluable commentary written
by Cardinal Ratzinger which accompanied the secrets release.
The book also contains a photocopy of the original *Third Secret*
text written in Sr. Lucia's own handwriting.   **$14.99**

Toll-Free (888) 654-6279 or (412) 787-9735 www.SaintAndrew.com

St. Andrew's Productions Order Form

Order Toll-Free! 1-888-654-6279 or 1-412-787-9735
Visa, MasterCard Accepted!

_____	Call of the Ages (Petrisko)	$12.95
_____	Catholic Answers for Catholic Parents	$ 8.95
_____	Catholic Parents Internet Guide	$ 3.00
_____	Face of the Father, The (Petrisko)	$ 9.95
_____	False Prophets of Today (Petrisko)	$ 7.95
_____	Fatima Prophecies, The (Petrisko)	$19.95
_____	Fatima's Third Secret Explained (Petrisko)	$14.99
_____	Finding Our Father (Centilli)	$ 4.95
_____	Glory to the Father (Petrisko)	$ 8.95
_____	God our Father Consecration Book	$ 3.75
_____	Holy Spirit in the Writings of PJP II	$19.95
_____	In God's Hands (Petrisko)	$12.95
_____	Inside Heaven and Hell (Petrisko)	$14.95
_____	Inside Purgatory (Petrisko)	$10.95
_____	Kingdom of Our Father, The (Petrisko)	$16.95
_____	Last Crusade, The (Petrisko)	$ 9.95
_____	Mary in the Church Today (McCarthy)	$14.95
_____	Miracle of the Illumination, The	$12.95
_____	Prophecy of Daniel, The (Petrisko)	$ 7.95
_____	Prodigal Children, The (Centilli)	$ 4.95
_____	Seeing with the Eyes of the Soul: Vol. 1	$ 3.00
_____	Seeing with the Eyes of the Soul: Vol. 2	$ 3.00
_____	Seeing with the Eyes of the Soul: Vol. 3	$ 3.00
_____	Seeing with the Eyes of the Soul: Vol. 4	$ 3.00
_____	Seeing with the Eyes of the Soul: Vol. 5	$ 3.00
_____	Sorrow, Sacrifice and the Triumph	$13.00
_____	Saint Joseph and the Triumph (Petrisko)	$10.95

Cassette

_____	Mary, and the World Trade Center	
	(2) 40 minute talks on one cassette	$10.00

Name:_____

Address:_____

City:_____St____Zip_____

Phone:_____Fax_____

Visa/MasterCard_____

Exp. Date_____Total Enclosed:_____

PLEASE ADD SHIPPING/TAX
$0-24.99...$4.00, $25-49.99...$6.00, $50-99.99...$8.00, $100 + Add 8%
PA Residents Add 7% Tax

OR MAIL ORDER TO:

St. Andrew's Productions
6091 Steubenville Pike, Unit #1, Bldg. 7
McKees Rocks, PA 15136

www.SaintAndrew.com